My Birthday Is on Saturday

ALSO IN THE MATHS FICTION SERIES

SUMMER IN NUMBERVILLE
BY *SOPHIA ASMAH*

My Birthday Is on Saturday

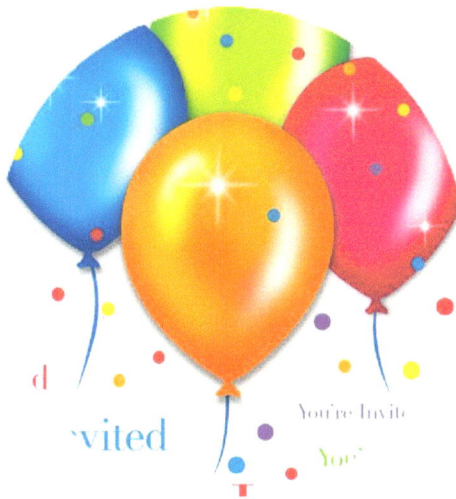

SOPHIA ASMAH

MATHS FICTION SERIES

SOPHIA ASMAH PUBLISHERS
Accra, Ghana

Published by Sophia Asmah Publishers
Email: sophiaasmahbooks@gmail.com
Facebook: Sophia Asmah Books
Twitter: @Sophia Asmah Books
Instagram: @SophiaAsmahBooks

To Isabel
my daughter

ACKNOWLEDGEMENTS

Thank you, first of all, to God for your never ending guidance and eternal mercy. I never thought writing would give me such great joy but it does.

A special thank you goes to my daughter, Isabel. She has always been my number one cheerleader and my invaluable critic.

I am very grateful to Lynn, who told me to reach a wider audience with my writing and never stopped encouraging me.

Also, thank you to Doris who kept telling me to write children's stories and never stopped asking 'have you written?'

Finally, thank you to everyone who has read anything I have written.

CONTENTS

CHAPTER ONE
No maths. It's about my birthday!

My least favourite subject is mathematics. I do not like it!

Mum says I do maths everyday and I don't even realise it.

"Really?" I asked.

"Yes!" she responded firmly. "I will remind you whenever you do a maths equation," she assured.

I wondered how and when I have been

doing math equations and I didn't realise.

I know I do maths in school. This year, my teacher is Miss Ruth. She gives me maths homework so I know I do maths in the classroom and for homework. For me, that is where my maths ends.

I was in bed while having the conversation on math with Mum. Therefore, I may have fallen asleep thinking of maths. Maybe I even dreamt about maths.

"Oh no!" I exclaimed.

I woke up on Saturday morning excited that it's a weekend and I had no school. Then, I remembered my birthday was a week away. We will organise a party on that day.

I will help Mum with the preparations for the party.

I have to make a list of nine (9) friends who will come to the party. I wonder if everyone will be able to come. I hope so.

First, I must check the list so that I give my friends the invitation cards at school on Monday.

"Where did I put the list?" I said out loud while I looked around my bedroom.

I found the list on top of a pile of my homework books on the desk. I grabbed it and run downstairs to find Mum.

On Saturday mornings, she was either doing some gardening or preparing breakfast. Mum is fond of making a cup of tea for herself first whiles she makes breakfast. I thought I would try the kitchen first.

"Mum, where are you?" I shouted.

Mum always says I don't need to shout

her name since she is always within a short distance from me. But I still like to shout her name so I only have to say it once.

"I'm in the kitchen. You don't need to shout," Mum responded.

I told you she would say that.

"Good morning Mum. I can't wait for us to talk about my birthday party! I have my list here," I said. And I went jumping all over the kitchen with excitement.

"Good morning to you too. Sit down. Have your breakfast and then we will talk about your party. I know you can't wait," Mum said calmly.

I am so excited about my birthday party

that I forgot to tell you my name.
I am Maria. I am 6 years old and I have
an older brother, Jacob, who is in college.
My dad is a pilot and at the moment he is
flying to China.

Dad always sends pictures of the cities
he goes to and I always look forward to
them. We also communicate through

video calls a lot so I get to see his face. Yet, I miss him!

Jacob loves art and that is what he is studying in college. This is a picture he drew of our family.

I am home with Mum a lot of the time

and for this birthday it will be Mum and I enjoying my birthday party. I will definitely leave Dad and Jacob some of my birthday cake.

And now back to the breakfast and my favourite cereal - cornflakes. I love eating my cereal with a lot of milk. It is only on weekends that I can take my time to eat my cereal because I do not have to rush to school. This is another reason why I love weekends.

I also forgot to mention what Mum does. Mum has a huge bakery where she makes all kinds of cakes. You name it; she makes it. I love visiting Mum's bakery. The bakery has its own funny name - 'Yummy.'

CHAPTER TWO
Friends and pizza

"Maria!" I heard Mum call out.

"Where could she be now?" I wondered.

I finished my cereal and washed my bowl. Then I went to the living room and there was Mum in the sofa, with her reading glasses on.

Mum had her notebook on her lap and her favourite white pen in her right hand. Her tablet was also on the sofa. I sat next to her and I could feel my excitement building up again.

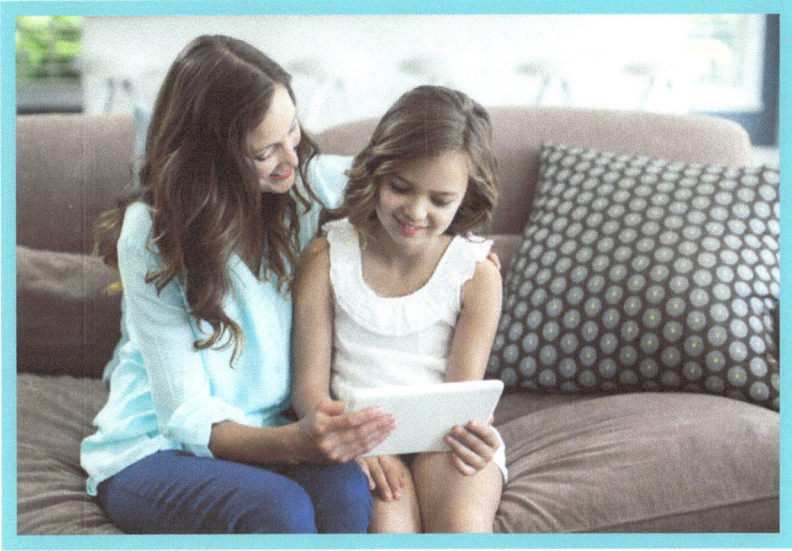

"Let's look at the list again," Mum said with smiles.

I guess she was getting excited too or maybe she was just happy to have me sit next to her.

Interestingly, I had made my list of nine (9) friends who would come to the party.

I wondered if everyone can come. I have to check the list so that I give my friends the invitations on Monday.

These lovely friends made it into the 'List of Friends:'
Jane
Mark
Samuel
Joseph
Chantelle
Alisa
Joan
Catherine
Peter

As we went on and on with the plans, Joan's mum called to say Joan cannot come to the birthday party because she has to visit her grandparents. This means I had to take out Joan's name from my birthday invitation list. I was left with eight (8) people on my list but I needed nine (9). Mum says we should be ten (10) kids at the party including me. So I have to add 1 more name to the list.

"Let me see," I whispered. "I will ask Jackson to come to my birthday party," I told Mum.

"I will call Jackson's mum to confirm if Jackson will be able to come," Mum assured.

I think it will be a good idea to have birthday cake, fruit punch, pizza, cupcakes, chicken and chips. In case a vegetarian attended, we should get plain pizzas as well as pizzas with meat.

Mum says she will make phone calls to

confirm who will want pizza with meat and pizza with no meat.

Afterwards, I left to play some computer games. This is why I like Saturdays. I am allowed to play games. Hooray! Thirty minutes into the game, I heard the call.

"Maria!"

"Yes Mum," I replied.

Mum had just finished with the phone calls. Let me go and continue with birthday preparations.

"Maria," Mum called. "Jackson's mum said he can come to your party next week so we have nine (9) friends coming to your party. When we add you to the list there will be ten (10) children."

"Yay!" I shouted.

List of Friends

Jane

Mark

Samuel

Joseph

Chantelle

Alisa

~~Joan~~   Jackson

Catherine

Peter

Mum said Chantelle and Peter do not eat

meat so we have to order pizzas without meat for two children.

"I didn't know they are vegetarians," I said.

"I am happy they will be coming to my party nonetheless," I said with a grin on my face.

"So let's decide on the food since we are talking about pizza at the moment," Mum said as she started writing.

"Each large pizza can be divided into 8 slices and each slice will be big enough for each person," Mum said.

Mum continued slowly, "We have 2 children who will eat pizzas with no meat. Therefore out of the 10 children, there will be 8 children left who prefer meat pizzas. So if we order 1 large meat pizza, which gives 8 slices, each child will have 1 slice of meat pizza."

"Then, for Chantelle and Peter, we can order a large pizza without meat which divides into 8 slices. After we give Chantelle and Peter a slice, how many will be left?" she quizzed.

I thought about it and said, "Six."

"This is because 8 slices take away 2 slices and you are left with 6 slices," I boasted.

"That's excellent," said Mum. "You have told me the right answer. There will be 6 extra slices for anyone who wants more."

Mum is always happy when I get things right.

CHAPTER THREE
Fruit punch and cupcakes

"Now, what about drinks?" Mum asked.

"Fruit punch, fruit punch...please," I kept repeating.

"Okay," said Mum. "Fruit punch it is."

"Each person will have 2 small cups of fruit punch. So how many cups of fruit punch do we need for 10 children, who include you?" Mum asked.

"There will be 10 of us and each of us

will get 2 small cups. That will be 2+2+2+2+2+2+2+2+2+2. That is a lot of numbers to add together, Mum," I complained.

Suddenly, I remembered Miss Ruth taught us about multiplication.

I asked, "Mum, do I multiply 2 by 10 to get the answer?"

"Yes," Mum said.

"Then the answer is 20," I shouted.

"Well done," said Mum. "The answer is definitely 20."

"Cupcakes Mum," I reminded her.

"They can each have 2 cupcakes...," Mum stressed.

"Twenty," I shouted before she could finish talking.

We both laughed. I knew Mum was going to ask me how many cupcakes we would have to buy. Since I had calculated 2x10 for the fruit punch, I knew 2 cupcakes for 10 children will also mean that we would need 20 cupcakes.

Mum smiled and said she would take care of the decorations and the give-aways for the party.

"I want to help with that too," I requested.

"Okay, we will go to the shop and pick out balloons, streamers and birthday banners," Mum agreed.

I love Mum. She always puts a smile on my face.

"Maria, so you see we have done a lot of math problems whiles preparing for your birthday party? What do you think? Maths is not so bad, is it?" Mum enquired.

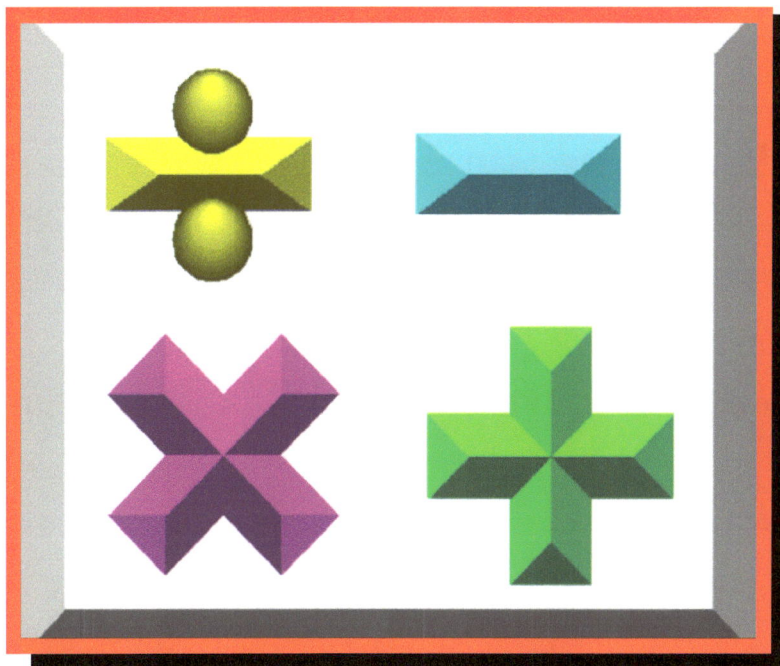

I sat and thought about it for a moment. Mum was right. I added, subtracted, multiplied and divided while discussing the preparations for the birthday.

"You are right, Mum. I think I like maths now. I have been doing maths without realising it," I laughed off.

She laughed too. I am sure she didn't expect what was coming.

"But please can I have a party every week? That will definitely help my maths," I added.

Mum just smiled and said, "I don't think so but I'm happy you like maths a bit better now."

"It will soon be lunch time but maybe we

can discuss a few things before then," Mum said.

"There is still quite a bit of organising to do. We still have to think of the birthday party games," Mum added. "I think I will leave that to you to plan and you can tell me which games you have decided on."

"That's easy," I shouted.

I was already thinking of all the games we could play.

"Musical chairs, freeze dance and pin the tail on the donkey!" I said jumping up and down.

"I have to practice my dance moves," I thought to myself. "This party is definitely going to be a lot of fun."

I was jumping around so much I didn't hear Mum saying something. She seemed to be talking in a louder voice now so I stopped jumping around to listen to her.

"Thank you for standing still. So as I was saying, I know musical chairs but not the other two games. Please explain them," Mum enquired as she walked to the kitchen.

I decided to follow her so that I could get a drink from the fridge. All that talking had made me thirsty.

"Now what should I have, apple juice or orange juice?" I asked Mum.

"You always like to have orange juice so

why not have apple juice this time? What do you think?" Mum suggested.

I decided to have some apple juice even though it wasn't my favourite. I took 2 glasses and poured apple juice for Mum and I.

"Here you are Mum," I said as I gave her

the glass of apple juice.

"You are such a lovely daughter. Thank you for the drink," Mum said. "All these birthday party discussions have made me thirsty as well."

We sat down at the table to drink our glasses of juice. Then we continued with the discussions.

"Now, which should I explain first? Freeze dance or pin the tail on the donkey?" I asked.

CHAPTER FOUR
Freeze dance

Then the door bell rang.

"That must be Joan. Her mother said she would bring her to spend the afternoon since she won't be able to attend your party," Mum said.

"We both forgot she was coming," I said laughing.

"Mum must also be getting into the birthday mood because she never forgets anything," I thought smiling.

Mum went to open the door and she was right. It was Joan and her mother at the door.

"Thanks for having Joan over for the afternoon," Joan's mother said.

Mum replied, "It is always nice when Joan comes over to play with Maria."

"We'll see you in the evening. Bye!" Mum waved.

Joan came in and Mum went back into the kitchen to prepare lunch. She said I could discuss the party games with Joan since she might also have some good ideas about them.

I went to the living room with Joan and put on the television. I tuned to my favourite kid's channel.

Then I turned to Joan who was sitting on the carpet. She said that was her favourite position when watching television. So I joined her on the carpet.

"Now Joan, this is what I think for the party games: musical chairs, freeze dance and pin the tail on the donkey," I said. "What do you think?"

"Freeze dance is a bit like musical chairs isn't it? So maybe we could leave that out and just have musical chairs," Joan said.

"It is not the same though. In freeze dance, when the music stops everyone is supposed to freeze. Anyone who is still moving will be out of the game," I explained.

"So if there are ten of us in the beginning, when the music stops if two people are moving then those two have to go out of the game leaving eight people," I continued explaining.

"Do you understand now? Ten minus two will equal eight," I continued.

Now, I stopped talking so that Joan

could ask any questions she had.

"I think I understand," Joan said. "So when there are eight people, if three people are moving when the music stops, then the three people will be out of the game and five people will be left. Eight minus three will give you five."

'You are right. This will go on until there is one winner," I said. "I know I'm not a good dancer so I have already started practising my dance moves."

We both laughed at the thought of me dancing already with seven more days to go.

"Your dance moves will be perfect by Saturday. I'm sure," Joan said trying to convince me.

I smiled at her. I really couldn't wait for Saturday.

"Let me get you a drink. Do you like apple or orange juice?" I asked Joan.

"Apple juice, please," she said.

"That's what we were also drinking before you came. I will get you some," I said and dashed to the kitchen.

CHAPTER FIVE
Pin the tail on the donkey

"Guess what?" I asked Mum when I got into the kitchen.

"What is it Maria?" Mum asked.

"You won't believe I was doing maths again when I was talking about the games with Joan," I said, sounding surprised. "I never thought I did maths so often."

"Really?" Mum looked pleased.

"Yes. I was describing freeze dance to

Joan and I was subtracting numbers to explain the game," I said as I started to practise my dance moves.

"That is very good. From now on, you will notice the times when you do maths. Remember I told you it isn't that bad," Mum said.

I grabbed a glass and poured some apple juice for Joan. I decided to tell her about my afternoon of maths with Mum.

I knew she didn't like maths too so I am hoping I can tell her about maths just like Mum had done.

"A good way to start will be to tell her the times we talked about maths when we were talking about freeze dance," I thought.

"Joan, have your drink," I said.

"Thanks," said Joan.

"My mother said fruit juice is better than soda so she doesn't buy soda anymore," Joan added.

"I told Mum that we should have fruit punch for the party. That will be better than soda. Won't it?" I asked Joan.

"My mother said all the fizzy drinks are too sugary so fruit punch is good," Joan replied.

"What was the other game you mentioned?" Joan asked.

"Pin the tail on the donkey," I said.

"There is a picture of a donkey on the wall and every one takes turns to pin the missing tail on the right place, on the donkey. The person who pins the tail closest to the right spot wins," I explained.

I saw Joan was laughing and I wondered

what was so funny.

"Why are you laughing?" I asked Joan.

She said I couldn't hear her as she joined in with the explanation of the game and that is what was making her laugh.

"Remember we played it at Chantelle's party last month?" Joan asked.

Now it was my turn to start laughing.

"I know I get very excited whenever it's my birthday but this time I am forgetting a lot of things," I thought whiles I was still laughing.

"You will remember to save some cake for me. Won't you?" Joan asked looking a bit sad.

"I will make sure your piece of the cake is the first to be saved. Don't worry," I said, hoping that would make Joan happy again.

"Thanks," Joan said beaming.

"Mum," I shouted. "I'm starving."

Then I remembered Mum said I shouldn't shout her name. I covered my mouth and started walking to the kitchen.

"Oh no!" said Joan. "You are in trouble!"

"Sorry Mum," I said when I got to the kitchen.

"Please, Mum is lunch ready?" I asked in a low voice.

Mum laughed because she could barely hear me.

I didn't want to give her a reason to say 'No Party!'

"Yes, lunch is ready," Mum said.

"Have you finished talking about the party games?" Mum asked.

"Yes we have," I said. "Freeze dance and pin the tail on the donkey."

"Then we are nearly finished with the preparations. Please call Joan," Mum said

I ran to call Joan for lunch knowing that my birthday party will still happen on Saturday.

We spent the rest of the day playing 'hide and seek' and running around in the garden. We also read some comic books.

Joan's mother came for her in the evening and with all the running around we did, I knew I would sleep early.

"I always have a lot of fun when Joan comes over to play. I will ask Mum when I can also go to Joan's house," Maria thought.

CHAPTER SIX
Invitation cards

Monday always comes very quickly and this Monday was the same. I always wondered why the weekend could not be three days instead of just Saturday and Sunday.

I woke up and dressed very quickly because I knew I had the invitation cards in my bag. I had to give them to my friends.

"I hope everyone is in school today," I thought.

When I got to school everyone was there except three friends; Mark, Alisa and Jane.

"Maybe they are just late and they will come later," I thought as I gave everyone else their invitation cards.

I checked to make sure I had given everyone their cards and when I counted, I had three left.

"Nine minus three will give me six," I thought as I did the calculation.

Since I had three cards left, I knew I had given out the right number of cards. I checked again to make sure the three cards had Mark, Alisa and Jane's names on them and those were the cards left with me.

I settled down for the first period with a smile on my face. Usually, I don't smile during the first period, which was maths, but today was different.

Since Mum's explanation that I do maths everyday, I felt better listening to Miss Ruth, my maths teacher.

Just as the class was about to start, Jane, Alisa and Mark walked in. They came with the school bus which delayed that day.

"I will give them the invitation cards during snack," I thought. "Otherwise, I will disturb the class if I gave it to them now."

$$2 \times 3 = 6$$
$$OR \; 2 + 2 + 2 = 6$$

Miss Ruth walked in and she said she would be teaching division. Immediately,

I thought of pizza and dividing it into 8 slices for my party.

"Maths is not that bad but I wonder if we will have pizza for supper later in the evening," I thought as I tried to pay attention to Miss Ruth.

Finally, it was time for snack. I took the remaining three cards out of my bag and gave them to Mark, Alisa and Jane.

"I hope you all come on Saturday. There will be a lot of fun," I said to them.

"Yes! I know I am coming," said Jane.

"I will also be there," Mark said.

Alisa also said her parents will bring her to my party.

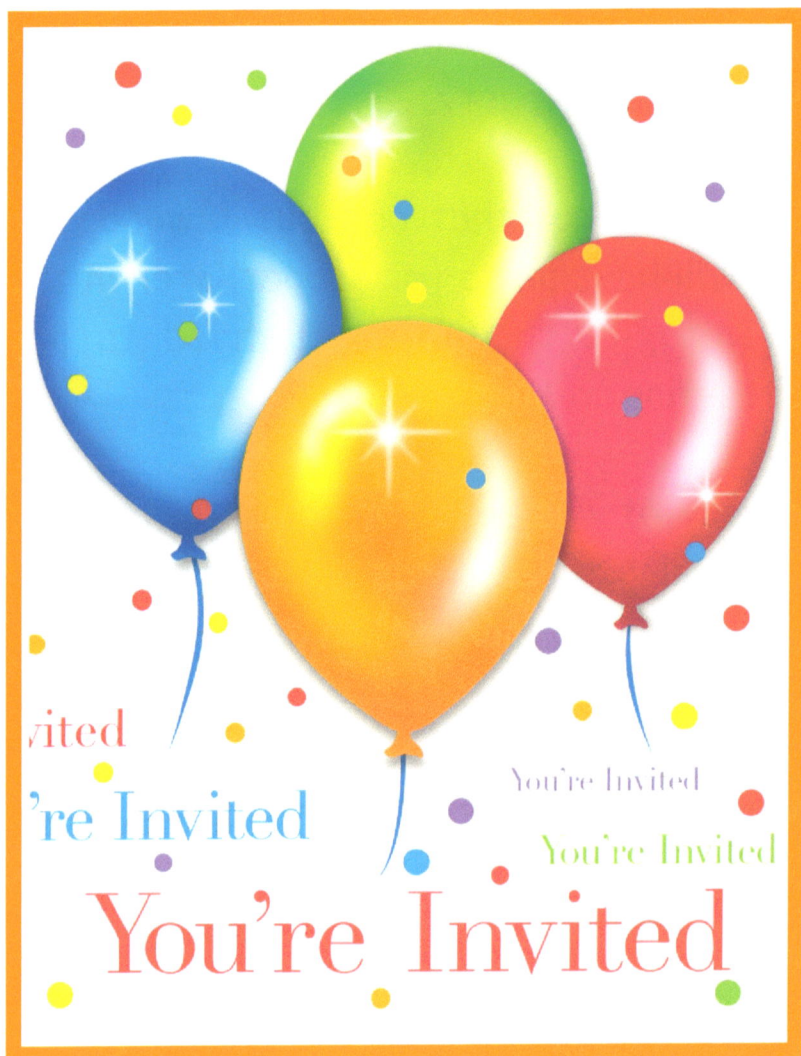

"This was great. Everyone had their invitations and everyone promised to be there," I thought.

"Five more days," I said aloud as I counted the days to Saturday.

CHAPTER SEVEN
Decorations and birthday cake

Mum picked me up at the end of the day and I couldn't wait for her to ask me about maths.

After talking about other things, she finally asked "How was maths class today?"

"Excellent," I said. "It was easier sitting through the lesson because I found it more interesting."

"What did you study?" Mum asked.

"Division," I replied. "And I immediately thought of pizza and the party."

"We will have pizza for supper since you mentioned it," Mum smiled.

I was very happy.

"I will call and order it when we get home. But on the way home, we should stop and buy the decorations," Mum said. "I don't want to leave everything to the last minute."

The shop was on the way home which was good.

Mum said she had found some balloons from Christmas so we only had to buy one packet of birthday balloons to blow up on the day. We found one packet of eight orange birthday balloons which should be enough for the party.

We also bought two big banners with 'Happy Birthday' printed on them. One will be in the garden and the other will be in the living room.

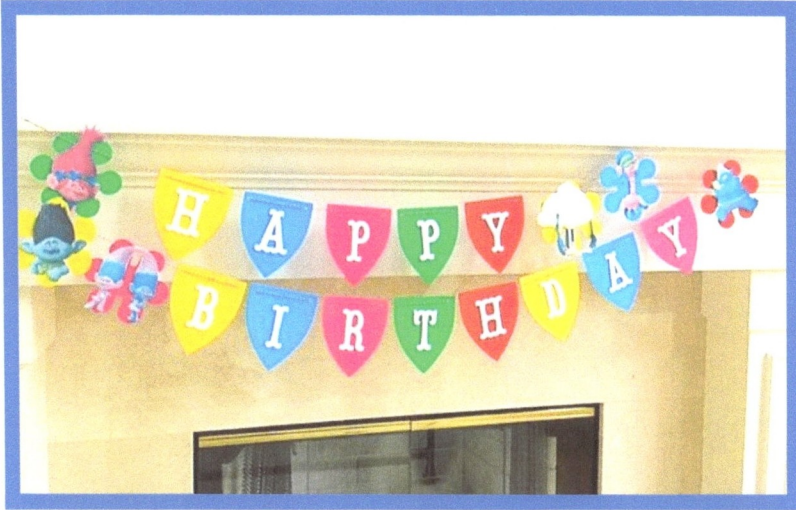

"Please let us get spray streamers," I said.

"I saw some on the other aisle," Mum said. "Please go and get four cans so that if there are any left over, we can keep them for another time."

"I'm not sure any will be left," I thought.

We got to the payment area and the items totalled $14. Mum gave me a $20 bill to give to the lady. She asked me how much change the lady would give us.

"Six dollars," I said. "Because twenty minus fourteen is six."

"That is right," Mum smiled.

"So please check the money when she gives the change to you," she added.

I felt proud when the lady gave me the change and I gave it to Mum, after I had checked it. I was happy she had allowed me to pay for the decorations.

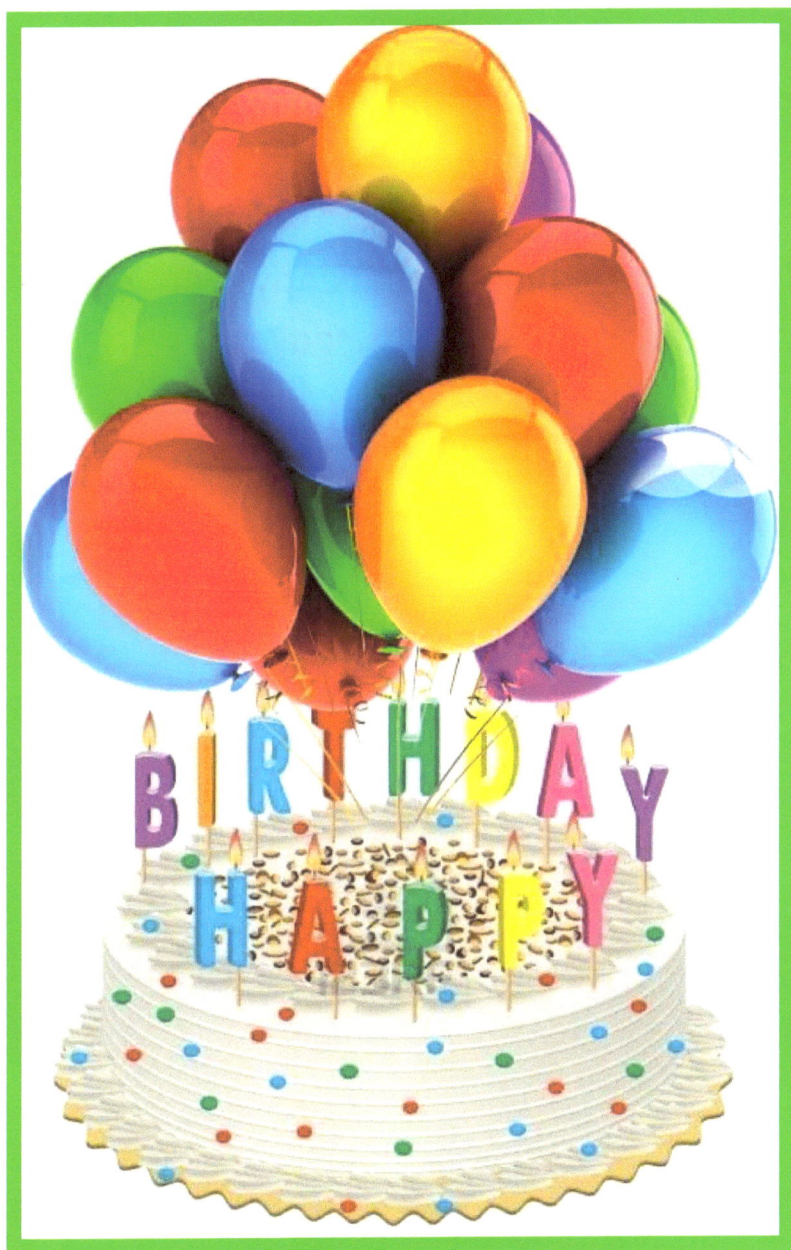

As we walked back to the car, Mum said that the driver from 'Yummy' will deliver my birthday cake on Saturday morning.

Now everything was ready for my 7th birthday party on Saturday.

THE END

www.ingramcontent.com/pod-product-compliance
Lightning Source LLC
LaVergne TN
LVHW010028070426
835513LV00001B/5